EATING

John Gaskin

Series consultant
Dr Alan Maryon-Davis

Franklin Watts
London New York Toronto Sydney

About this book

This book is all about food and eating. It tells you about many different types of food and what happens when you eat. On pages 28 and 29 there are projects and things you can do. If you see a word printed in **bold** letters, this means that you will find more about the word in the Glossary on pages 30 and 31. You can also look up the word in the Index on page 32.

First published in Great Britain
in 1984 by
Franklin Watts Limited
12a Golden Square
London W1

First published in the USA by
Franklin Watts Inc.
387 Park Avenue South
New York
N.Y. 10016

Published in Australia by
Franklin Watts Australia
1 Campbell Street
Artarmon, N.S.W. 2064

UK edition: ISBN 0 86313 143 3
US edition: ISBN 0-531-04632-X
Library of Congress Catalog
Card Number: 84-50021

Printed in Belgium

Illustrated by
Elaine Mills

Designed by
James Marks and Steve Wilson

YOUR BODY

EATING

Contents

The food you eat

Can you remember what you had to eat and drink yesterday? Did you have any of your favorite foods? Was there anything that you didn't like very much?

There are many things about food which you may like or dislike. There is the taste, which may be meaty or sweet, bitter, sour or salty. There

is also how it feels – it may be soft, hard, chewy or crunchy. And the food itself may be raw, fried, baked or boiled.

You may think you would like to eat only your favorite foods all the time. But you would soon miss the different flavors, feels and colors you get from a mixture of foods.

Where food comes from

◁ This picture shows where some foods come from. Butter and cheese are made from milk from cows. Wheat is ground to make flour for bread. What other foods from animals and plants can you see?

All foods come from either plants or animals. Fruit and vegetables are plant foods. So are **cereals**.

Animal foods that you eat may come from land animals like sheep, cows and chickens, or from sea animals like fish.

Some of the foods that you eat come in cans or packages. The raw food may first have been processed by a factory so that it no longer looks the same.

Feeling hungry

When you haven't had anything to eat for a while, you start to feel hungry. This is your body's way of telling you that it needs food. When you have eaten a meal, the feeling goes away.

Feeling thirsty is your body's way of telling you it needs water.

▽ Your stomach may start to rumble when you feel hungry. The smell and sight of food can make you feel like eating. The taste is also important.

You can go without food for a long time because your body can store food and use it later. But you can't manage to go without water for very long.

This is because you lose water all the time by sweating, by breathing and by going to the bathroom.

▽ Sometimes you have a choice of foods. Do you ever try anything new? If you do, you might find you like it.

Why you need food

▽ Food provides your body with all the building blocks you need to grow.

The food you eat contains many important things which your body needs.

One of these is **protein**. Your body uses it for growth and to repair and replace damaged and worn-out parts.

Food also contains **sugar**, **starch** and **fat** which your body uses for

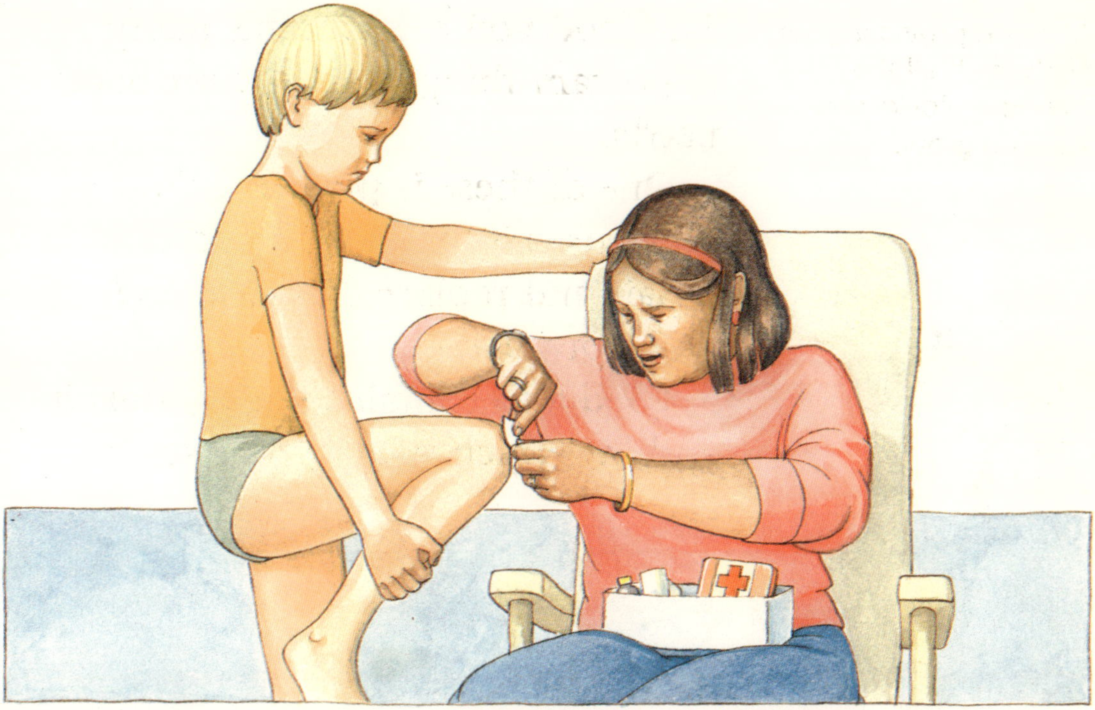

energy. You need energy for all the movements you make and to keep warm.

There are also **minerals** and **vitamins** in food. You only need very small amounts of these. Minerals are used for building bones and teeth as well as in other parts of the body. Vitamins are needed to help keep you healthy.

△ Sometimes you damage a part of your body. It maybe a cut, a graze or a broken bone. The food you eat gives your body the materials to repair the damage and heal the wound.

Putting food in groups

▽ Get to know which groups different foods fit into. Eating a variety of foods from each group will help you keep healthy.

To stay healthy you need drinks and different types of food. There are hundreds of foods, but they can all be put into just four groups.

One group is made up of grain products, which are cereals and bread. These come from plants. Pasta and rice are in this group.

Another group is fruits and vegetables. Like grains they come

from plants, but are more watery.

Foods which come mainly from animals and some special plants make another group. All meats, fish, poultry, eggs, nuts, peas and beans are in this group.

Milk and all the different products made from it, like cream, cheese, yogurt and butter make up the last food group.

Not all foods are good for you

There are some foods which you should try not to eat too much of.

Eating or drinking too much sugar is bad for your teeth and may make you fat. Candy, chocolate, cakes and most carbonated drinks and sodas all have lots of sugar in them.

You should also try not to eat too many fatty foods. That doesn't just

▽ If you get hungry between meals, try eating fruit instead of candy, cakes and cookies.

mean fried foods, fatty meat and butter and margarine. Fat is also used to make cakes, cookies, ice cream and pastry. Too much fatty food can also be bad for your heart.

Think about the food you eat. Do you have a lot of sugary and fatty foods? Can you try to stop eating some of them?

A healthy diet

▽ The food people eat is not the same all over the world. But there are always foods from the different groups to eat. Asian people eat rice as a starchy food while those in Europe and North America eat potatoes and food made from wheat.

How can you be sure that what you are eating is keeping you healthy?

Make sure that the food you eat comes from all four groups. Then you will be eating a healthy mixture, as well as having foods that don't all have the same feel and flavor.

Don't eat too much! Eating more food than your body can use will

make you fat. And a lot of salt is not good for you, so don't put too much on your food.

Try to eat plenty of food with **fiber** in it. Fresh fruit and vegetables, cereals, beans and peas all contain fiber. Fiber helps to keep everything you eat moving easily through your **digestive system**.

▽ This girl is a vegetarian. She doesn't eat any meat. She can still keep healthy by eating foods from the grains and fruits and vegetables groups, and eats only milk, cheese and eggs from the animal food group.

What happens to food?

You probably forget about your food as soon as you have swallowed it. But that is really only the start of a long journey during which your body takes everything it needs from the food.

Your body can't use the food you eat just as it is. It has to be changed. The way that your body breaks down food so it can be used is called **digestion**.

▽ Your teeth bite off food and grind it as you chew. Your tongue helps to move the food around and mixes it with saliva.

Digestion starts in your mouth. There the **teeth** cut, rip and grind food too big or tough to swallow. A liquid called **saliva** is also added to soften and mix the food. The tongue pushes it to the back of the mouth. Then you can **swallow** it.

△ This girl is using a knife and food blender to chop up large pieces of food. She adds liquid to make it softer. This is what happens to food in your mouth.

The stomach

Where does food go after you have swallowed it? It travels down a tube called the **esophagus**. This tube can stretch so that bits of food of different shapes and sizes can be squeezed down it.

The esophagus leads from the mouth to the **stomach**. This is rather like a bag made of muscle. The food you eat stays in the stomach for a while before passing on to the next stage of its journey.

While the food is in the stomach, it is churned around, mashed and mixed.

Digestive juices are also added to

▽ Try pushing a ball along a tube by squeezing it with one hand. This is how muscles in your esophagus push food along. This movement of the muscles is called **peristalsis**.

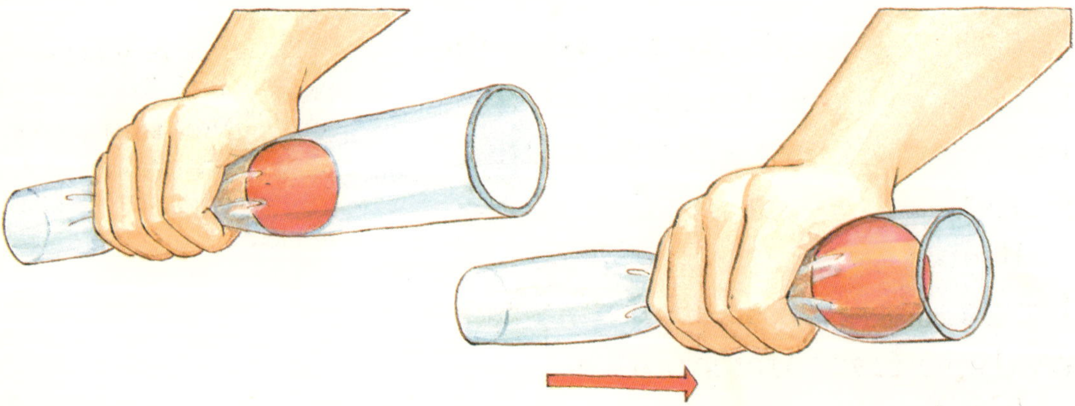

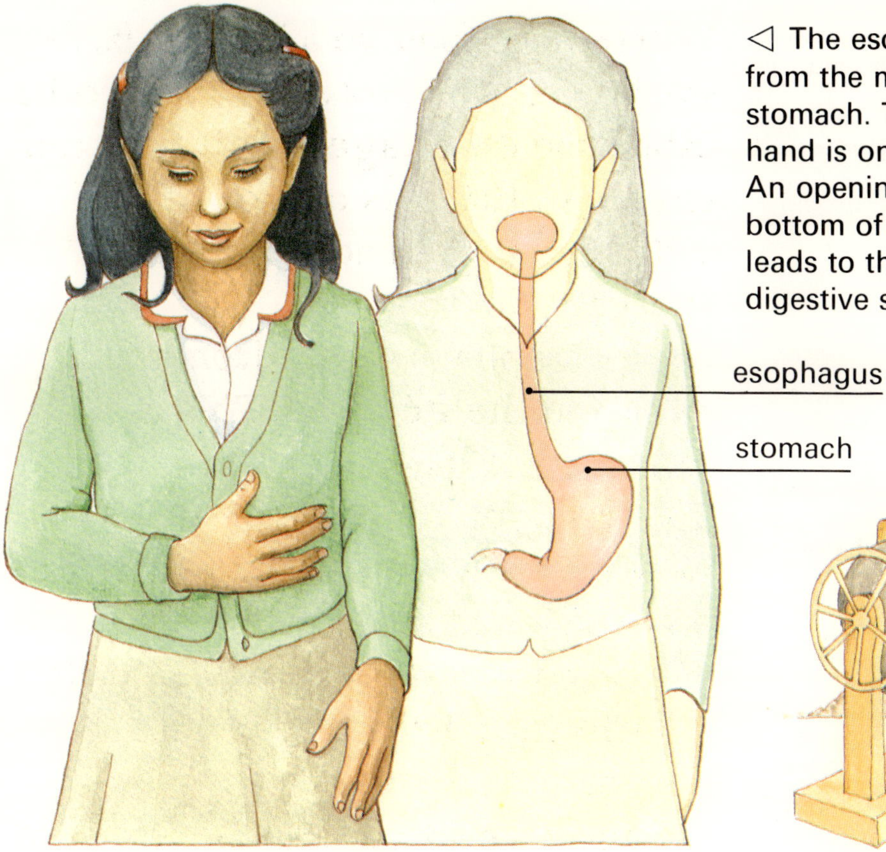

◁ The esophagus leads from the mouth to the stomach. This girl's hand is on her stomach. An opening at the bottom of the stomach leads to the rest of the digestive system.

△ The stomach acts like a mixer. The stomach muscles move all the time so that the food and liquids inside are churned and mixed.

dissolve the food. By the time the food leaves the stomach, it has all been turned into a thick, mushy liquid.

If you eat a big meal, it can take as long as six hours before the food is ready to leave the stomach.

The intestines

When the liquid food leaves the stomach, it goes into a long tube called the **small intestine**.

This is where digestion is completed. All the parts of the food your body needs can now pass through the walls of the intestine. They go into the blood, which carries them off to be used or stored.

The remaining food passes into the **large intestine** along with some water. Most of the water is removed in the large intestine leaving a semi-solid waste. You pass this out when you go to the bathroom.

▽ The small intestine is very long – about 13-23 feet. It is called small because it is narrow. Stretched out like a hosepipe it wouldn't fit in your body, so it is coiled tightly.

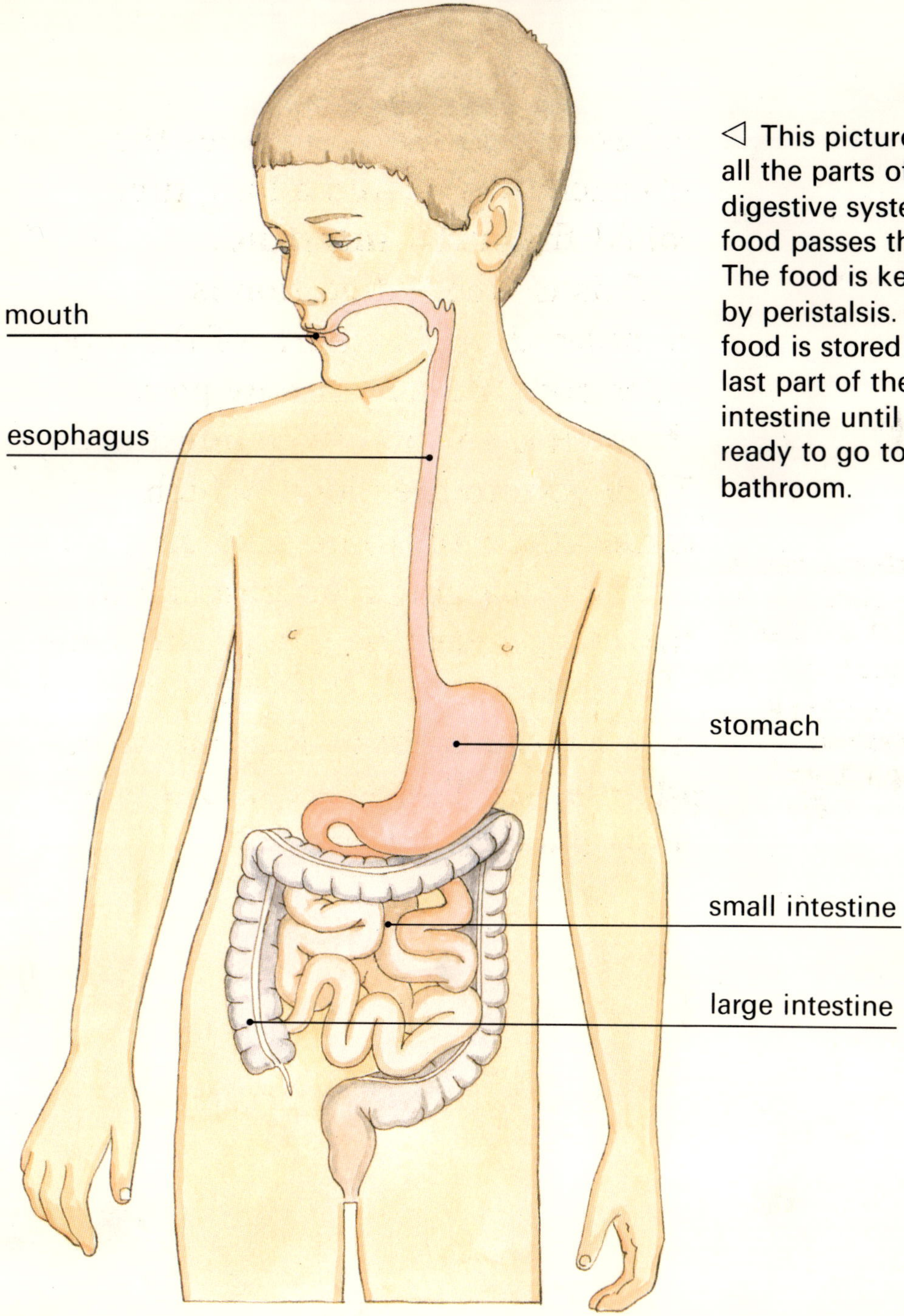

◁ This picture shows all the parts of the digestive system which food passes through. The food is kept moving by peristalsis. Waste food is stored in the last part of the large intestine until you are ready to go to the bathroom.

How your food is digested

1 Food can take 12 hours or more to go through the digestive system. This is what might happen to a mouthful of food chewed at 12 o'clock.

2 Food enters stomach about 5 seconds after swallowing.

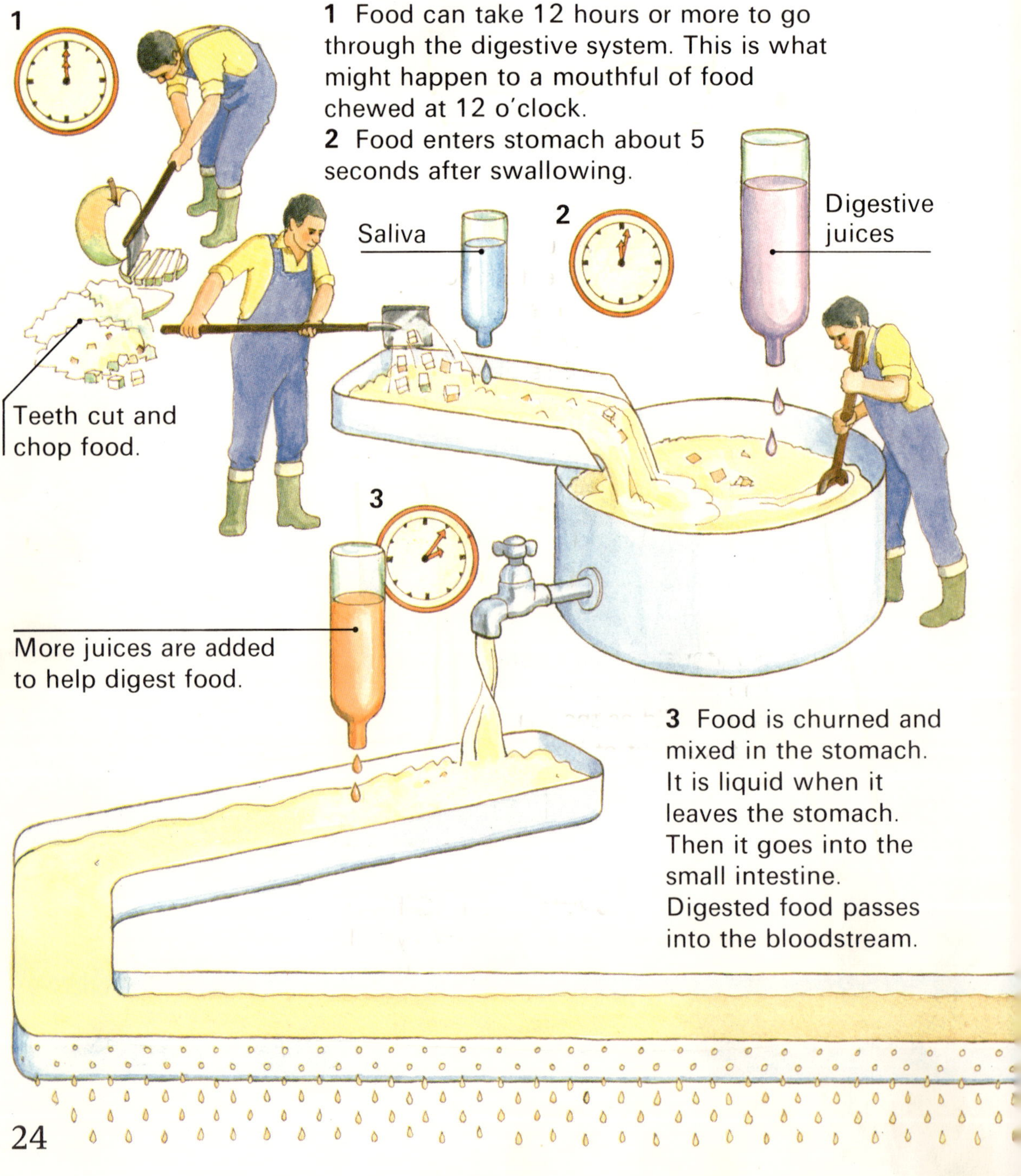

3 Food is churned and mixed in the stomach. It is liquid when it leaves the stomach. Then it goes into the small intestine. Digested food passes into the bloodstream.

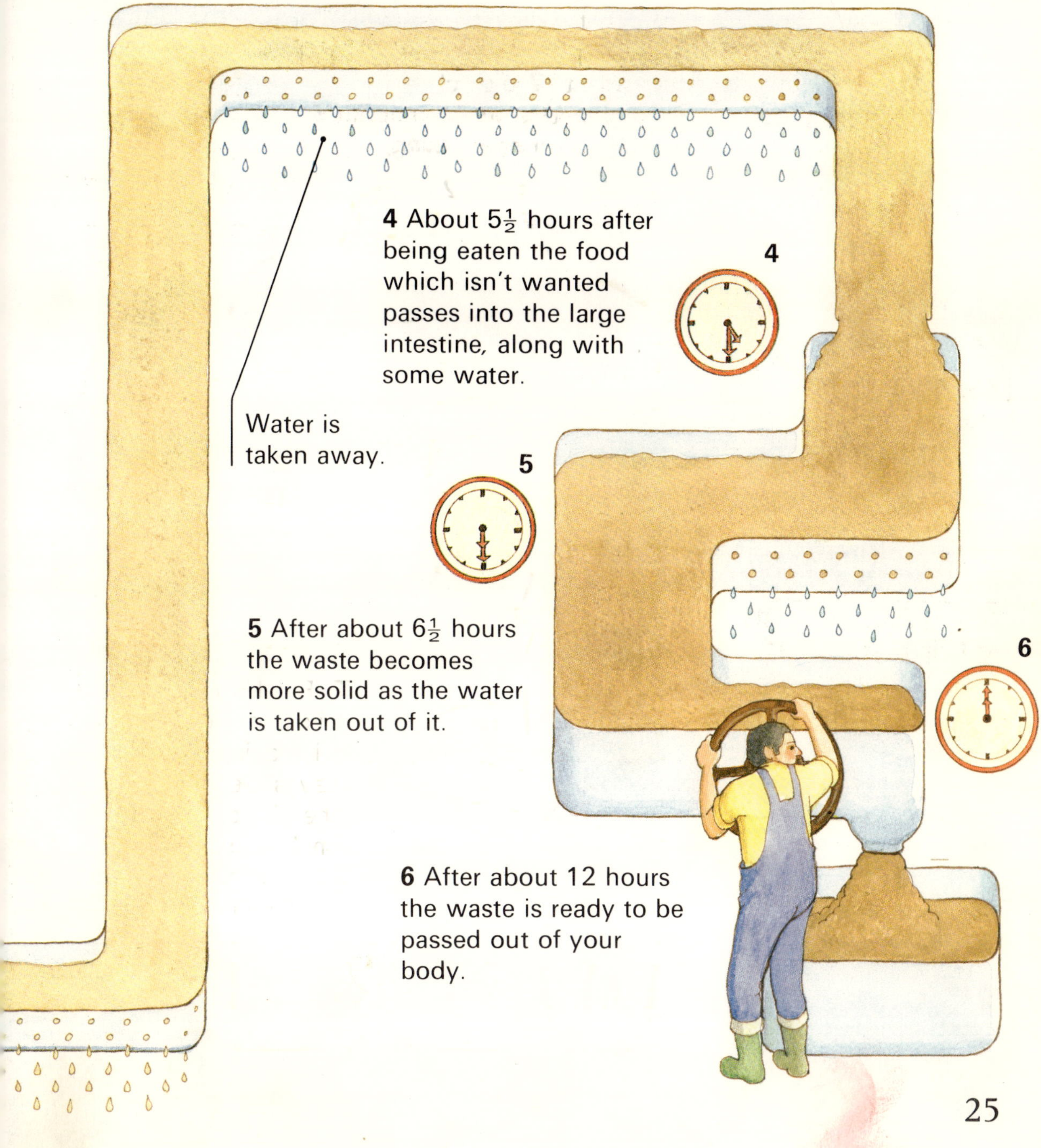

4 About $5\frac{1}{2}$ hours after being eaten the food which isn't wanted passes into the large intestine, along with some water.

Water is taken away.

5 After about $6\frac{1}{2}$ hours the waste becomes more solid as the water is taken out of it.

6 After about 12 hours the waste is ready to be passed out of your body.

Feeling sick

26 ▽ If you are sick, you will feel tired and will need to rest. Don't eat anything until you feel better, but drink small amounts of water.

Have you ever had an upset stomach or been sick and wondered what was happening?

When you are sick, the food that is in your stomach comes back out. It is pushed out by strong movements of the stomach muscles.

The food looks, tastes and smells different from the food you may have eaten. This is because it has been mixed with digestive juices in your stomach.

If you don't feel well, or have eaten food which is not fresh, you may also have diarrhea. Your intestines try to get rid of the food as quickly as possible. So the food you have eaten passes through your digestive system much faster than usual. This means that the water is not taken out of the waste which is why it is more like liquid than solid.

△ Sickness and diarrhea may be caused by germs which can spread from one person to another. You may not know if you have the germs so you should *always* wash your hands after going to the bathroom and before eating.

Things to do

1 Keep a record of all the food and drinks you have in a day. Do this every day for a week. At the end of the week look at everything you had. Which of the foods came from animals? Which of the foods came from plants? How many of the plant foods were grains and how many were fruits and vegetables?

Now you can see what you ate over a whole week, is there any group of foods which you are having too much of? Is there a group you are having too little of? Are you eating a lot of fatty, salty or sugary foods? Is there sugar in the drinks you have? Are there any changes you would like to make to the food you eat?

2 See what happens to different foods in your mouth. Try apple, cheese, bread, potato chips, yogurt, meat. Try a bit of each food in your mouth in turn:
Does your mouth water?
What does the food feel like?
Can you describe the flavor of the food?
Does the food go soft without chewing?
Which food takes the longest before going soft?

3 Plan a meal of your favorite foods. Does it include food from more than one group? If not, how could you make it better?

Glossary

Cereals These are all grain foods like wheat, corn, oats, barley and rice. Wheat is ground to flour to make bread and pasta. Oats are used in oatmeal. Corn is used in many breakfast foods. Rice can be boiled, fried or used in sweet puddings.

Digestion The breaking down of the food in the body so that it can be used.

Digestive juices Liquids that are added to food in the mouth, stomach and small intestine to break it down so the food can be used by the body.

Digestive system All the parts of the body through which food passes after it has been eaten.

Esophagus The tube which joins the mouth to the stomach.

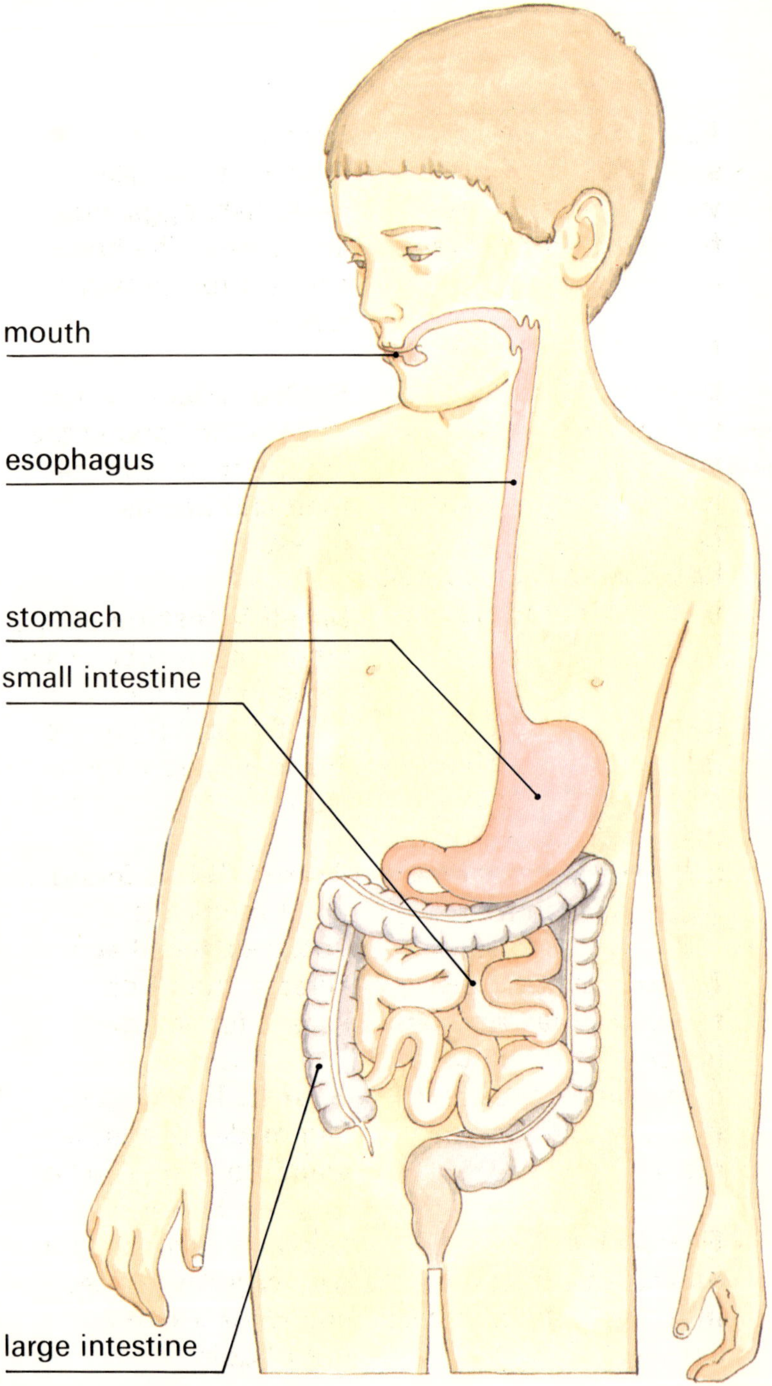

Fat One of the substances in food which the body uses for energy; it is stored in the body.

Fiber This is found in plant foods. It doesn't get broken down and used by the body but it is important because it helps digestion and keeps waste soft so that it is easier to move and pass out.

Large intestine The part of the digestive system where the unwanted waste becomes more solid as water is taken from it.

Minerals These are found in small amounts in food. They are used in building bones and teeth, growth and repair.

Peristalsis The movements of the muscles in the digestive system.

Protein This is found in many foods like meat, fish, eggs, nuts and beans. The body needs it for growth and repair.

Saliva A liquid which is added to food in the mouth. It softens the food and begins digestion.

Small intestine A very long, narrow tube where digestion is completed and the useful parts of the food pass into the blood.

Starch This is found in plant foods like potatoes, bread and cereals. Your body uses it for energy.

Stomach A stretchy bag made of muscle where food goes when it is swallowed. The stomach mixes the food with digestive juices and turns it into a thick liquid.

Sugar This is sweet tasting and is found in some plants. It is used by the body for energy. It can be taken from plants and made into crystals which are used in sweets and cooking. In this form it can be bad for teeth and can make you fat.

Swallow What you do to pass food from your mouth into the esophagus.

Teeth These cut, rip and chew food in the mouth. Cutting is done by the front teeth called incisors, ripping by the pointed teeth called canines and grinding by the back teeth called molars.

Vitamins These are found in very small amounts in food. They are important for many of the body's processes.

Index

PRINTED IN BELGIUM BY proost INTERNATIONAL BOOK PRODUCTION